Dear Helga and Ron,
God lives among us
each day! Jesus walks
by our side wherever
we go!
may these writings
somehow reflect that,

Walter Huber

1/5/99

GOOD STUFF!
Life . . . live every minute of it!

Walter Huber

VANTAGE PRESS
New York

Illustrations by Manni Ruhnau

FIRST EDITION

Copyright © 1998 by Walter Huber

Published by Vantage Press, Inc.
516 West 34th Street, New York, New York 10001

Manufactured in the United States of America
ISBN: 0-533-12431-X

Library of Congress Catalog Card No.: 97-90581

0 9 8 7 6 5 4 3 2 1

To my wife, Louise, our family, friends, and the people I've met along the way

Contents

Preface

Life is a GIFT! We may each think of it a bit differently, but most of us understand life was given to us and we had nothing to say about it.

Living life is another story. This part is completely up to us! We can make of living a mess or we can make of it a wonderful, exciting, and beautiful experience . . . for ourselves and for others.

GOOD STUFF! is simply excerpts, happenings, and bits of ordinary living. Some ups and downs, some tears, some laughter, some burdens to carry and some help from others to carry our burdens. A brilliant theme, however, seems to weave itself persistently through all these activities. It is that if we grit our teeth and get up out of the big soft chair and recognize that it's up to us, no matter what . . . it's a big beautiful world after all.

Like the subtitle says, "Life . . . live every minute of it!"

Enjoy! I'll be thinkin' about you.

—Walter Huber

GOOD STUFF!

And That Ain't Easy

Some people
have a good friend
a really good friend.

Everyone
would like to have a good friend
a really good friend.

A really good friend
is a rare treasure
more priceless
than diamonds or pearls

who's part of your life
and you part of his.

A friend
can be a mom or dad
a brother or sister
a wife or husband . . .
a stranger, and

friends can walk a seashore
at dawn or dusk
and never say a word
yet communicate
with every beat of their hearts
as they stroll quietly side by side
and

friends can laugh and squeal and shout
in the noisy throng
of fun seekers
at a crowded carnival
and

find in the excitement
a privacy of their friendship
as if they were alone
on a distant star.

Friends get angry
but never mad at each other
and

friends don't have to "make up"
to make up.

Friends
believe in each other
love each other . . .

not the love
of passion
but the passion of another love
a friendship love
a special love.

Friends accept each other
just as they are . . .

flat out
accept
and respect
and love each other
just as they are,
and

there's only one way
we can have a friend
a really good friend.

We each must be
a really good friend,

and,

that ain't easy.

Something Special for Tom

Tom and I were sitting on the rock at his lake yesterday. The sky glowed like a burning ember, a hint of sunset being lowered down on us. We talked some . . . we sat quietly some. Cattails guarding the shore of the lake swayed to the rhythms of the breeze. Many times in forty years we shared such magical moments.

Tom will be seventy in five weeks and I want to do something special for him. He has everything. What to do for someone like that? My thoughts wandered. In a quiet time, I looked over at him. He's a good-looking guy, strong Slavic features, bushy eyebrows, and thick dark tousled hair that matches his mustache and personality.

I decided to do a bust, a sculpture in modeling clay, as my "something special for Tom." (Later, it hits me—I don't know a thing about clay except to track it in the house. So . . . a bust of Tom? Yup! I'll give it a try.)

Tom called one day, "C'mon down to the shop and see my new automatic turret lathe. It's a beauty! We'll have lunch." He knew I'd be right there. I vividly recall his eyes as he came to meet me—they were dark brown, pupils tinged with blushes of green around the edges, piercing, vibrating with curiosity, observing with intensity. They glinted out excitement like sparks slashing into the air from steel being worked on a thirty-inch grindstone. He gave me a hug and pulled me to the new machine, "What do you think about this? Some beauty, right?" And it was. "This lathe will make parts accurate to a whisper of an inch. Some of these parts will go into brake systems of well-known cars." Tom loves to make things out of ordinary raw materials—the look on his face and the excitement in his voice tells you so. The sculpture must show this.

My first step is to get a book on modeling clay. I find one at the library. After studying "how to," I visit Morse Graphics Art Supplies. With the help of friendly people there, I gather up clay, some simple sculpting tools, and materials to build the pedestal. Back in my studio (corner of garage behind the lawn mower), I think more about Tom.

Suddenly I'm shaken. All these years and I don't even know if he has wrinkles. I really don't know a lot of things about him. I do know he has a "hundreds-of-acres" farm in mid-Ohio and that he's a successful businessman and that he's a wonderful guy to liven any occasion. And he's a mighty fine friend! But all these years and I don't know if he has wrinkles.

I begin to work. I make a full-size sketch of side view and front view from photographs. I mount an "armature" post to pedestal base. This will support a crude-shaped head out of chicken wire and the clay, as I apply it and sculpt it.

Tom's eyebrows are arched high, like he's surprised. Noticed this a long time ago. We were chatting out on his gravel driveway. There were only seven kids then . . . there are eleven now. One little girl was kicking gravel around.

"Please don't do that, Nancy," Tom suggested.

"I'm not Nancy," said the little girl as she kicked another stone.

"Well . . . don't do that, Janet," Tom, almost calmly, persisted.

Kicking one more stone quite deliberately, she replied quite deliberately, "I'm not Janet!"

More than slightly reddened, and also quite deliberately, Tom barks out, "Dianne, stop that!"

"I'm not Dianne, so there!" She grinned a sassy grin and heartily kicked a footfull of gravel clear across the drive.

Exasperated, with all the fatherly authority he could muster, firm, yet with a strained patience, Tom commanded, "Uh . . . well . . . whoever you are, don't kick the gravel anymore. I mean it! Don't!"

Wisely, she did stop. Never really knew which kid she was, but I did observe that Tom's eyebrows always had the surprised look.

I work the brick of clay to make it pliable and workable, like working bread dough. This is called "wedging," according to the library book. It is ready for modeling. I begin to apply clay to the armature.

Anthony Podovano in his book, *The Process of Sculpture,* discusses sculpturing in mediums such as: brass, iron, stone, marble, wood, and clay. He writes,

"Sculptors often use easy working clay to 'try out' their ideas before they tackle the brass or wood or stone." He tells us, "Clay became a 'thinking medium' for the sculptor." Interesting! According to Podovano, the "hands" and "hopefully the heart and soul" of the sculptor must show in his work.

Wedging and kneading. Reminiscent of days spent with Tom at his farm. Like working clay, soil must be worked to prepare it for planting.

One day at the "Big T," as Tom calls his farm, between mouthfuls of husky bacon, nest-fresh eggs, raw fries, and the awesome coffee of a farmer's breakfast, I asked, "Tom, tell me about working the soil."

"Better yet, I'll show ya!" he said. When he's enthused (and he almost always is), his eyes squint like he's looking into the sun . . . they are eager and dramatic. "T'day you and me are gonna work the ten acres behind the big barn. We'll be preparing the soil to plant experimental feed-corn. It's s'posed to have more nutrients and harvest out at more bushels an acre. And that's good! Put on some jeans and meet me at the tractors." And I did.

"We'll use the old Fordsons. Know how to run one yet?" I told him I did. He went on, "I'll plow because I can judge how deep a bite to take. Different soils have different curls. Furrows must be straight for cultivating and harvesting equipment. Takes practice. You're pulling the spike harrow to break up the curls on the piece I plowed yesterday.

"Okay. Mount your machine. Start your engine!" His face lit up like the headlamp on a charging freight train. Crinkles flowed out the corners of his eyes like water streams across a windshield in a bad rain. An impish grin shaped his lips. "All set? Let's go! Let's go! Let's go!"

As he pulled away, I realized his entire being participated in every activity. His face was a continuous reflection of what he was feeling. I smiled. How large his ears were, and how his thick curly hair, dark, not black not brown, camouflaged them . . . crazy mem'ry. Jaw, resolute determined as that of a defensive tackle, but, amusingly, jutting out over a slight double chin . . . and that's a crazy mem'ry.

I passed Tom as we made turns at the end of a furrow and he shouted, "Smell the fresh worked soil? Nothin' like it!" He was so right . . . soil's an honest, stimulating, pungent reminder of creation.

Memories refreshed, I work to shape the clay. I forget nose and big ears at this time. Working from front to back, using hands, ruler, caliper and paddle, I roughly model head and neck. I refer often to sketches and photos taped to wall of my studio (behind the lawnmower). I have Tom looking upward . . . because he's always alert, never misses anything.

Finished for the day, I wrap bulk clay in plastic

film, put it in an old coffee can, and snap lid on to keep moist. I cover bust with a wet towel.

Tom loved music. I'm sure he always will. He had a "big band" of his own during the thirties and forties. His fingers nimbly manipulated the blacks-and-whites of his accordion as he squeezed out a foot-stompin' "Beer Barrel Polka" or a heart-tuggin' "Stardust." His face changed with each mood, unveiling emotion and feeling completely. When in a "serious" mood, very few lines showed. When in a "satisfied" mood, a trollish grin came out and a soft glow floated in his eyes. When it was an all-out "spontaneous" mood, his eyes squinted almost shut and his grin burst into a contagious full-blown laughter that nudged his mustache up under his nose, and his entire face filled with lines, crinkles, and wrinkles! And they seemed to belong there.

Yes indeed, he had wrinkles! Still has!

I will try to capture his "satisfied" mood because his teasing grin and soft glow eyes say he's "ready for anything . . . and you better be too."

But Tom has another look that must also come through. His parents came from Yugoslavia . . . God only knows where that is now . . . and his face tells of the pains and the struggles, the joys and the wisdoms, the prides and the loves of that culture. Tom's look is at once inscrutable and yet revealing.

I wonder how I can capture these many facets in clay.

Here and there I add clay or take it off. I form the ears and nose and attach them. I sculpt slowly, letting Tom's face come out of the clay a bit at a time. It's taking patience and hands and modeling tools . . . but mostly patience.

The lump of clay is beginning to resemble Tom. Unbelievable! Remarkable! Vastly exciting!

Tom somehow can make any thing or time exciting. Like simply trudging the furrows of a matured corn field. He'd break off an ear of corn, "This one's ready. The silk tassel's browned and dry." He'd pull back some leaves and juicy kernels stared out at us. "See how the silk strands are between every kernel? They carry water to them. When kernels are fully formed and no longer need water, the silk drys and browns." His look showed wonder at every marvel of creation.

Tom loved dancing and parties. He loved rib roasts. He loved harmonizing with friends, singing the old songs he once played as a band leader. Yet, there'd be those times of an afternoon when he'd turn to me and coax, "Let's go down and sit on the dock and look over the lake. We'll chat for a spell. Okay?" And of course, it was okay.

We'd talk . . . we'd sit quietly. With a green fluorescence of head feathers, a white neck band, a rusty

breast, and a brilliant blue speculum (the patch of wing feathers that shows only in flight), a mallard would plop into the water. With a majestic flourish, a Great Blue Heron would silently glide to the water. A green frog would b'dunk somewhere among the swaying cattails. The haze of sun-warmed earth bathed by cool evening breezes misted the landscape into a serene Renoir painting . . . so gentle, so powerful. Finally I knew—this communing with mysteries of the ages, with pure truth of creation, with a friend of many sunsets and sunrises—this was Tom's "thinking medium."

More hours of scraping and modeling exposes an unexpectedly real likeness of my friend. The eyes do have that surprised look. Subtle lines, crinkles, and wrinkles do seem to belong there. A touch of the inscrutable yet emotional look comes through. This is going to work. I set the bust aside for a week to dry.

To finish the sculpture, I spray it old gold, like a treasure of the ages. Voila! It turns out a beautiful antique bronze . . . it surely is a treasure of the ages.

Tom will be pleased!

With the likeness carefully boxed and wrapped, I arrive on time for Tom's seventieth birthday party.

He "unveils" the sculpture. He pauses for a long time. Finally he turns his tousled head towards me, whisks away one tiny tear as his eyes said what words can't, and quietly struggled with, "Wally, you old son-of-a-gun! You . . . you old son-of-a-gun!

I wanted to do something special for Tom. I did! It turned out to be special for me, too.

Thanksgiving: A Reminder

It seems to me we need reminders to remember things, especially important things. Thanksgiving Day is a reminder to be thankful!

You'd think we'd remember to be thankful without the reminder of Thanksgiving Day, or to treasure those we love without Sweetest Day, or to feel the intensity of birth without the reminder of a birthday. You'd think we'd remember all of these happenings and many more, without a reminder. You'd think so, but we can't or won't. Most of us need and appreciate reminders. They serve as does the string tied around a finger as a reminder to bring milk and bread home from the store.

And there's nothing wrong with that. After all, we need calendars to know what day it is.

Thanksgiving Day reminds us to pause a bit and think deeply of what we are giving thanks for.

We are happy about the day. The banging of pots and pans, the cut cut cut of busy knives, the bubbling kettle of soup, the perkling coffee pot brewing its darkish concoction. Oozing out of this activity come sounds of laughter and giggling and shouts and whispers . . . young eager voices absorbed in intense conversations, and underlying chuckles and contented murmurs that grandmas and grandpas make.

The whole world seems misted with wonderful aromas and steamy smells. Turkey is browning comfortably, biscuits are rising and baking, pumpkin and mince meat pies are set out for cooling. Noodly brothy fog blurps from the cover of the churning kettle of soup, an almost-taste of tart cranberries, sniffs of gravy and mashed potatoes, golden yams with a marshmallow baked on here and there.

It's such a wonderful day, indeed, to be happy in!

As the day slowly sees dawn brighten to midday and begin its gentle fading through twilight into the dark of night, somewhere during that time we search our hearts for the deeper meanings of this day of thanksgiving. The search begins simply with, "Thank you for your bounty, Lord, and for the crop, and for the harvest!" There the simplicity gracefully, almost unnoticeably, becomes an exciting awareness of vast and deeper meanings.

We hear the God of the great sky and the great water and the great land tell us to subdue the earth, to bring the land under cultivation. We see the peoples of the earth, then and now, do this. With extraordinary toil and effort, physical tiredness and pain, the forests are cleared, rocks dragged to one side or another, and the crust of the land is tilled to offer life and strength and growth to seeds sown within the furrows.

The planting is finished, but the toil is not. New shoots sprouting into life require vigilant care, must be fed and cultivated, must have enough sun but not too much, enough rain but not too much, must be protected from storms and marauders.

No one can do all these things . . . yet those who

cultivate the land that we may have our "daily bread," they do do these things. These people must have a source of courage and strength beyond themselves, to draw upon . . . a God, a Highest Being, a Mighty Power.

Finally comes fall, Mother Nature carefully tinting the leaves with smudges of rainbow colors, the grains of the fields proudly wearing their golden tints of ripeness, and harvest time. Sweaty? Yes. Itchy? Yes. But reaping of the harvest is a celebration, a prayer of gratitude, a grin and laughing eyes.

The climax of this mighty effort to subdue this earth, to bring the land under cultivation, is to sit down to our dinner of Thanksgiving. In what way we can, we try to grasp the full meaning of God's bounty, His generous gifts, His blessings upon us. And when we pray, each in our own way, "Thank you for the bounties we are about to receive!" we somehow glimpse the great wisdom—"bounties" include skills and talents, courage and strengths, guidance and blessings bestowed upon all of us to enable things to be accomplished.

Thanksgiving Day reminds us to think deeply of what to be thankful for, and to whom to be thankful.

It Would Make a Difference

What if your life were exactly as you wished it were? Or everything in the world like you thought it should be? Or people just like you wanted them to be?

Do you really think it would make a difference? That you'd be happier? Life would be easier? People more exciting because they were like you?

Joy of living is because of the unexpected: differences add richness and an exhilarating dimension to relationships, they dispel life's boredom and dullness.

The older person says, "You wouldn't understand. You're too young." The younger person says, "You wouldn't understand. You're too old." Kind of humorous!

The woman says, in a not-too-complimentary way, "Yup! Just like a man." The man says, in a not-too-complimentary way, "Yup! Just like a woman." And that's kind of humorous!

These remarks are rooted in a belief that if things are "different" than we think they should be, they're unacceptable, and people different from us should change to become like us. Such thinking misses thrills and rewards to be found in differences. Natural and man-made creations that are the most different make up the list of "Wonders of the World."

If we'd each be different for a change and accept

the fact and welcome the existence of differences, if we'd each enjoy every moment of differences in things and people . . . it really would make a difference. It really would!

Terror on the River

Thank God for grandchildren—they keep us acting twenty years younger and inspire us to be able to do so . . . at least most of the time. Thank God for grandmothers—they do anything for grandchildren . . . even to fighting terror on the Mohican.

I was scared! My Louise (Gramma) was terrified! But she hung in there. We'll probably do it again—if the grandchildren coax a little (maybe a lot). But, we'll do it differently.

Here's what happened . . .

What a day! Seven A.M. A crisp August morning. We and our four grandchildren are throbbing with excitement as we pile into the car. We're going canoeing on the Mohican River . . . canoeing for the first time ever. Gulp!!! With a great "Yay!" we head south on I-71 toward Loudonville, Ohio, and the Mohican River.

Gentle hills roll out playfully before us. White farm houses are a fresh white. Red barns are a fresh red. We breathe pungent smells of pine trees, outdoorsy fragrances of new-mowed hay, and sturdy odors of working barnyards. Happy white clouds bulge through blue skies and sunshine floods the landscape as far as we can see.

Nothing . . . not one thing . . . even hints of the terror we'll find on the river.

Grandchildren, oldest to youngest: Jen, college

bound, tries to be grown-up, but the little girl peeks out delightfully here and there; Teece, an unusual name for an unusual young lady, is the carefree one; Andy is a six-foot-five lovable giant who goes along with anything (that is, almost anything); Jesse, slender as a green bean pod, is our thinker.

Free-spirited Teece, large blue eyes sparkling and voice alive with a spontaneous elation, bursts out with, "It's gonna be an 'up' day today, Gramma!" Her grandmother smiles over at me.

Andy blurts out with, "Hey! When're we gonna eat breakfast? I'm starved!"

Jen jibes, "Andy, you're always starved."

I wheel off the Interstate down a country road that pokes through white pine woodlands where Delaware Indians hunted for food and Johnny Appleseed roamed. We come upon Mohican Lodge snugly relaxed among magnificent water hemlocks with branches drooping gracefully as a ballet dancer bows. We, not reluctantly, join "starvin' Andy" for breakfast.

"Gramma, are you really goin' with us?"

"Yes, Teece, I'm really going with you."

"But, Gramma, you can't swim. You can't even float."

"I'm afraid of the water, but I want to be with you guys. OK?"

"It sure is OK! I'll take care of you." Teece is slim trim. She glides through water with the elegance and confidence of a sleek yacht.

Starvin' Andy's hunger being satisfied for now, we head the last few miles to Loudonville. I check with Louise: "Are you sure you want to do this? Are we biting off more than we can chew?"

"I'm sure. I'll be fine. I'll be with *you*, ya know."

Louise and I clamber out at the Mohican Boat Livery nervously trying not to show how nervous we are. She is trembling.

We go with: "Beginners should take the two-hour trip to Frye's Landing." I MasterCard the transaction and glance at the posted "SAFETY TIPS" . . . I should've studied them.

Zoom!!! The kids leave the launch ramp, girls in one canoe, boys in another. We're still collecting our paddles and life jackets. Louise, stiffly brave, wonders, *Gosh, how muddied these life jackets are. Ugh!*

Tense as Kentucky thoroughbreds being coaxed into starting gates, we proceed to embark (an experience in itself). The canoe rocks. Louise is tossed into her seat at the bow and shouts, "Oh, God!" Our paddles are uncertainly poised and the dock guys launch us . . . we hear another, "Oh, God!"

Suddenly we're in the middle of the Black Fork of the Mohican River. People hereabouts call it Muddy Fork, and it is. Flows six miles'n hour. Runs mostly twenty inches deep, fishin' holes ten feet. Black Fork joins Clear Fork four miles down stream. Trees and bushes along the bank, and the sky, are populated by chirping, warbling, and cawing birds.

We don't see or hear this living panorama. We're uncomfortably busy trying to steer and paddle . . . or paddle and steer . . . however it's supposed to go. Current tugs us one way, paddling tugs us another. Kids are out of sight around a bend. The more we struggle to keep up, the faster out of control we are.

With a roar, "white water" is ahead. Frolicking ten-inch-high sprays of water look to be three feet high. They must look ten to Louise.

"Wally! Wally! Get to shore. I can't go through there. I really really can't. I'll drown if we go through there!"

No way can I get to shore before we reach white water. (*Dear Lord, I need your help—NOW!!! No time to explain.*) "We'll be OK, Louise. Put the paddle under the seat. Just hold on! Hold on tight! Don't get up or anything!"

Intense fright quivers her lips and stabs out of her eyes. My spine chills. My heart beats drummer's jazz rhythms. Time abruptly pauses for a moment . . . an eternity, to be exact.

With skill beyond my ability, I conquer the intimidating white water. Inward I'm shaking. Outward, "There we are. Not bad. You did great, dear. Great! Really!!!" She is as white as the rapids' froth. Shivering, she bravely patterns her lips into a kind of smile.

Paddles are somewhat effective now. We can clumsily change direction, though not exactly where or when we want. We see the kids where Muddy Fork flows into Clear Fork and we try to get to them.

Nearing the junction, I realize the current, faster and stronger because of heavy rains, will pound with a force like a firefighter's nozzle stream against the far bank of Clear Fork where a huge water hemlock is down in the river. Ahead another "Frye's Landing" couple is trying to make the bend. I figure to pass between them and the tree. I call, "Louise, paddle harder! Paddle harder!" Seems to be helping, but a glance tells me they are heading toward us. Our speed has increased. We are racing to the giant hemlock.

All at once the tree and the canoe and the river crush in on us. Louise pierces the air with a shriek of total terror, "Turn the boat! Turn the boat! Turn the boat!"

With a bit of desperation myself, I cry out, "I can't! I can't! I can't!" We're like a torpedo about to slam into a destroyer.

"Oh, God! Oh, God!" squeezes out of Louise as she drops her paddle and hangs on . . . literally for dear life.

The other canoe rams our bow and veers off down stream. We hit the tree, which is half under water, and the rounded bottom of the canoe rides up on the trunk and dumps us into the river. I fall out against the tree and discover we're in a ten-foot fishing hole. Louise shrieks an unmistakable sound of "fright" as she is catapulted out to the other side of the tree.

"Oh, God! Oh, my God! Wally! Wally! Wally!"

I stretch out. I grab her hand. "Hold on to the tree. You're okay. You have a life jacket on. It's deep here."

A gym bag with camera and thermos falls out. . . . I can't reach it. We lose a paddle . . . I can't reach it. My one arm tries to hold up the canoe, but the current keeps pushing it down on Louise's head. We are frightened. Terror is lashing out at us. We can't free ourselves. My right elbow is torn and bloodied. Edges of the tree bark chew into our arms like a rabbit chews into lettuce. Louise is being torn away from the tree. The undertow's trying to pull us to the bottom. Suddenly, two men beach their boat, jump in to help us, and all I can say is, "I'm Wally. This is Louise."

"I'm Frank. That's John. We've got the boat." They pull the boat up on the tree and dump the water.

"Gramma, Gramma, I'm comin'!" Teece gurgles as she swims upstream toward us. The "Frye's Landing" people had hollered, "Your grandparents are in trouble back there!"

"Oh, Teece, I'm so glad you came back!"

Teece firmly puts a loving arm around her grandmother. "Everything's okay now, Gramma. I'm here. Just hold on to the tree."

John reaches down as Teece boosts Gramma onto the hemlock and into the canoe. Frank and I balance the boat. I get in. Louise strenuously, though reluctantly, understands we must cross to "Mom's Hot Dawgs" refreshment stand to get off the river. Teece will swim at the bow to steer. I will help with one paddle . . . I hope.

We exchange "Thanks!" and "You're welcome!" as Frank and John slide the canoe into the water. Louise clenches the sides again. We swim, paddle, and white-knuckle our way across to Mom's Hot Dawgs place. The other kids paddle to meet us, shouting, "We've got your paddle!" On landing we pry Gramma's hands free and pull the canoe high on shore for pick-up later.

We are dripping Muddy Fork, ridiculously be-draggled, exhausted, and hungry. Terror's grip is relaxing a bit.

Teece says, "Gramma, I've never seen you so dirty before!" And Gramma is . . . she and her life jacket are so "muddied," so "ugh!"

In my pocket I find some wet dollar bills. I ask the "hot dawg's" lady, "Are these any good?"

"Sure are. I jus' clip 'em on the rack to dry. Happens all the time. What'll ya have, mister?"

I look to Louise. She says, "A Bloody Mary . . . make it a double!"

Sitting on rough benches, hot dawgs, dollars, and minutes later, Jesse, our thinker, turns to me and says, "Hey, Grandpa, ya should've taken a rubber raft."

Louise glances in my direction and bravely, as if it's a prayer, breathes, in almost a whisper, "Hey, Grandpa, next time we *will* take a rubber raft!"

He Touches Me

He . . . touches . . . me.

He touches me!

God touches me this morning!

It was at sunrise and
The great ball fiery red and
The feeling of blanket warmth and
The hug that squeezed the chill of morn . . .

He . . .
God . . .
God touches me this morning!

He . . . lifts . . . me.

He lifts me!

God lifts me this day!

The sky is grumpy and
The chill wind dreary wet and
The droop within my heart and
The sun peeks out, the rainbow too . . .

He . . .
God . . .
God lifts me this day!

He . . . blesses . . . me.

He blesses me!

God blesses me this day!

The house is homey and
The windows shine so bright and
The woman's eyes are flashing and
The world's great joys we're fully sharing.

He . . .
God . . .
God blesses me this day!

He . . . loves . . . me.

He loves me!

God loves me today!

It is at sunset and
The moon is full and jolly and
The child tucked safe in bed and
The soft "I love you, Mom and Dad."

Me . . .
God . . .
God loves me today!

He . . . touches . . . me.

He touches me!

Yes, God touches me!

He has all day long and
The many many endless ways and
The tears that turn to laughs and
The reaching out to keep me whole . . .

He.
God.
Yes, indeed! God touches me today!

This Man and His Guitar

This man and his guitar
I've heard so many many times . . .
in many many places
in so many many climes.
Sometimes he's black, and then again,
he's sometimes just as white,
and sometimes ev'ry other shade
somewhere 'tween day and night.

The man can sad and lonely be,
no matter how he tries . . .
his shredded heart a-bleeding shows
through teared and misty eyes.
His arms reach out to all the world
for someone he can hold.
His mind and thoughts are filled to brim
with stories to be told.

But then he reaches down to get
his fav'rite old guitar . . .
he hugs it close and strums away
of mem'ries from afar.
His eyes begin to sparkle bright,
and joy fills full his heart.
His life renews through ev'ry vein
and ev'ry spirit part.

Another time this man can have
a burst of happiness . . .
his grinning lips and crinkling eyes
a-spreading cheerfulness.
It seems that never can he be
downhearted, sad or blue,
his thrilling joy so fills the air
with such a rosy hue.

And once again he reaches down
his old guitar to fetch . . .
his nimble fingers send the notes
as if a star to catch.
The melody takes buoyant flight
that leaves the lark below,
and has the trees and fleece white clouds
a-swaying to and fro.

O Lord, O Lord, I too can be
in pain, afraid, alone . . .
I too can feel delight and laugh,
and muse on things unknown,
but Lord, O Lord, where's my guitar,
that come the storm or sun,
I can, as he, strum hurt away
and be with joy as one?

Request Form for Holiday Flo

Please print clearly. Your messag
Fund is $10.00 and donations

Contributors to Flower Fund may take

Name _____

flwrordr.sam(Deacon file)

Mark "I

Suggested Donation for Flow

If you are making a gift to either Fund below, do

name of the

Fund	Yes?	
"In His Name"		_____
Permanent Memorial Endowment		_____

hurch
Endowment

orialize loved ones. Our church offers
embrance will be listed in the printed
ions with the form below is **December 1,**

day plants for our sanctuary—the suggested
nase a manageable number of plants of
cel. Although this means donors will not be
ast Christmas Eve service we will still
eeding a lift in spirit!   (An added bonus:
ng our holiday flowers, that money will be used
has donated flowers!)

ppeals for emergency assistance, special mission
congregation. Donations to the IHN Fund may be

—all contributions build the Fund and generate
rmanent Memorial Endowment Fund may be made in

Beating the Blues

The sky has fallen in! My brain's a kaleidoscope of my life's colorful bits and pieces, making crazy reflected patterns every time I try to think. I feel like a kamikaze pilot wearing sunglasses looking through a shattered windshield, heading in an unknown direction not knowing why.

The blues? I shake my head . . . *I* don't get the blues . . . blues are for other people, not for me.

For weeks I live with believing I'm in charge of my brain—but I'm not. "God, what's happening?" I stagger to the kitchen sink, stick my head under the cold water to wash a few cobwebs. I lift my dripping head and stare right at the solution.

A precious masterpiece in an ordinary frame, hanging on our kitchen wall. It's not done in oil, or acrylic, or watercolor . . . but in Crayola. A creation of free verse written to us years ago by granddaughter Teece, then eight. It goes like this:

If you suffer from
loneliness then,
go to your closest
friend's house, cousin's
house, etc., and ask them
to come over, or call them
on the phone.
And your problem
will be gone!

An exquisite understanding of an emotional state and its absolute solution: "Lonely" will go away if you do something about it. Lonely . . . blues—the same thing. A lightning bolt crashes through the mess in my head. I must heal *myself* . . . family and friends will help . . . but *I* must do it. I must heal myself.

Collecting my thoughts, I ponder as I walk to City Hall to pay a water bill. Morning sun bounces through winter-bare branches of tall oak trees splashing a special spring warmth into my life. I need that!

Mayor Martin fills his office with genuine friendliness. As I pass his door, he waves me in and we chat a bit. Gives me a chance to ask, "Mayor, do you ever have 'blue days'?"

"Sure do! About ev'ry two weeks."

"How d'you know when you're havin' the blues?"

"When a whole lot of things pile on me and I can hardly breathe. When I'm not getting anywhere." He leans across the desk, and with intensity, continues, "In my work I don't have a sense of accomplishment. A carpenter can work for hours, then step back and see the cabinet he built."

The mayor puffs his briar. Curls of smoke corkscrew upward into nothingness. "When I feel down, I do three things. First I make a list of problems and concerns overwhelming me. Then I arrange them from most to least important. Finally, I set time goals and knock them off one at a time. However, I find it necessary to relax regularly as I proceed . . . in my garage I make wooden toys for kids. Kids love the toys! Toys are tangible. I can see what I've accomplished. Makes kids feel good. Makes me feel good. Real good!"

My problem is me. I'm drowning in self-pity. I never would have believed that. I return home and write my first list:

1. STOP THE SELF-PITY.
2. Spend less than you make . . . NOW.
3. You've taken too many projects . . . dump some.
4. Do more for others. They can use your help.
5. "Knock 'em off one at a time."

A schooltecher once said things I understand now. "Keep busy. Do things that require use of mind and hands. Give good attention to the job of the moment. *Like* what you do."

Days later, swallowing my pride in one big gulp, like taking cod liver oil, I ask my pastor for help. It's quiet here in church. It encourages thought and introspection. Jon, a fine young man of Generation Today, can tap his shoes to soft rock, yet sing a hymn with robust sentiment. His eyes glint of wisdoms and convictions; his welcome, sincere; his handshake, firm.

Jon's glad to see me, been worried. I explain. I ask Jon if he has blue days.

"Yup! I do. Blue days are part of life's healthy emotions, such as love or anger, and as such, blues must be understood, accepted, and dealt with."

"How d'you know when you have the blues?"

"Hm! That's a tough question." Jon takes a thoughtful pause. "There's no line to cross, no flares to signal you. It's important to somehow recognize the feeling . . . if you don't, you can't deal with it. For me it's like I'm walking around in a fog. Finally I say to myself, 'Uh oh, Jon, you're feeling glum.'

"But the blues aren't all bad." Jon continues. "It's good at times to be blue. I let myself feel glum for a while. Feeling sorry for oneself helps unload useless baggage of worrisome thoughts. It's a time I look around and see where I am, a mind-resting place. But, it's essential to understand I can't stay here, I can't wallow in the blues pit."

"How do you get yourself out of the blues pit?"

"Most important, I admit I'm in a blues mood. To strengthen self-esteem, I list positive things I've done. Then I get up and help someone. By the time I've worked with someone, there's no room left in me for the blues. No blues left in the person I'm working with, either. We both feel good about ourselves. And each other, too!"

Jon says blues happen to anyone, to not feel badly,

to not "stay wallowing in the blues pit," but to get up and help someone.

Granddaughter Teece is twenty now, lovely, vivacious and caring. Blue eyes flash a fiery spirit. Brown swirling hair. Manner, poised and confident. The little girl has become an exciting woman. Teece is such an up person . . . can she possibly have blue days anymore? I wonder?

"Teece do you have blue days anymore?"

"Do I get bummed out sometimes? Grandpa, of course I do!"

"How d'you know you are . . . mmm . . . bummed out?"

A puzzled look scurries across her face. "I just know. When I wake up, I just know. You don't hurt or anything, you just know!" She half shrugs and half smiles, like trying to figure out how the magician made the elephant disappear. "At breakfast, my parents ask, 'Are you okay, Teece? Do you feel all right?' Parents always seem to know. And at work, my friends ask, 'Hey! What's wrong, Teece?' By then I'm sure I'm bummed out . . . you call it 'havin' the blues,' Grandpa."

"Teece, 'bummed out' may be a better way to say it. So what d'you do now?"

"I'm quiet, stay by myself for a while, even at work. Don't want to get others in a bad mood. Same as a cold . . . you can pass it around, y'know. Then I want to do something, be with someone, go over and scrub Gramma's kitchen floor; or mow the lawn for the widow lady down the street; or help my neighbor paint a dining-room ceiling. It doesn't work 100 percent, but it gets me going—makes me feel better! And somebody else feels better, too!"

Most of us have blue days because something didn't go our way, or a task is tougher than we expected, or we've done some dumb thing. Who knows? But some individuals sink into a quicksand, a desolate swamp of sadness and self-pity . . . why? I ask myself, can I, with an optimistic and positive attitude, help others to "get up and do something" about the blues so their "problem will be gone"? I'm going to try.

Within a few weeks, I'm out of the quicksand and back on solid ground . . . with the help of God, loving and patient family members, and friends.

Yup! I'm beating the blues these days!

Once in a while, I'll do something special, like ask someone to walk with me along the lake shore or hike through the woods or across rolling farmlands . . . during a warm summer rain. Sometimes I'll be frivolous and buy a Boston strip steak or a wild tie or a silk shirt, unlike anything I would usually buy.

Occasionally I'll do something outrageously exciting—like going to a place by a river, or in a meadow, or high on a hill, just before dawn . . . and quietly watching nature's spectacular as the rising sun melts away the darkness from the sky!

Ode to Valentine's Cupid

Amid the swirling blowing
chill white snows of winter day
there breathes the warmth of logs aflame
and hearths at dance and play . . .
and bitter biting winds
of cold cold nights
bring fires of love
and Valentine delights.

And here and there do hearts entwine
alive with Cupid's bow,
who seek to bring a bit of heav'n
to grace this earth below . . .
Two loves ablend,
with joys of life o'erflowed,
to fill all souls
with music sounds untold.

Be thee, O Cupid, ever ever,
spirit of our loving hearts!

My Friend Jim

A hundred times I've walked this long long hall at the Veterans Administration Hospital since my best friend had his devastating stroke three years ago. I turn into his room. From his wheelchair he smiles a mechanical smile and struggles to wave his left hand.

"Hi, Jim! Do you know me?"

He answers, "Mon mon mon."

We've been friends fifty years. He had the laughing eyes and broad grin of his Irish father and the fine features and courteous manner of his English mother. He'd say, "My good looks and nut-brown hair are my idea, ya know!" He used words well and related pleasantly with people—valuable in his profession of "sales."

Years ago I'd phone, "Hi, Jim! Know who this is?"

"Yup! It's Walt. What's cookin'?"

Sometimes we'd sit around and talk, maybe argue. Other times we'd take in a vaudeville show at the Palace Theater or a baseball or football game at the Cleveland Stadium. Heading home one of us would offer, "Let's stop at Malley's Ice Cream Parlor for a tin roof sundae. My treat!" And we would.

This strong bond of friendship keeps me coming back to ask over and over and over, "Jim, do you know me?" I pray I'm the key that unlocks his shackled mind to free his thoughts for us to share again.

This exhilarating fall day is a great time to visit a best friend. I drive south on I-77 then east on I-480 to the Brecksville VA facility. Trees are casually daubed golden yellows and ruby reds and fiery oranges as though a leprechaun splashed around searching for his pot of gold. Brisk air floods my lungs awakening my very soul. All my heart strains to bring this fall magic into Jim's small room.

Jim's entire vocabulary includes his welcome "Mon mon mon!" plus, "Now now now," "Bam bam bam," and "Panna panna panna." Simple gestures mean "yes" or "no."

Bob comes in. A young nurse with hands and energy as full of caring and compassion as his heart must be, "Hey, man! Need anything?"

Jim replies, "Mon mon mon."

"All okay, huh. How about some water?"

Jim gets excited. "Now now now!"

Bob turns. "When he gets excited, means he wants some." Sure enough, a smile slides out of Jim's mouth when Bob brings fresh ice water.

Jim's eyes don't sparkle anymore . . . sometimes shine a bit, shrouded by deep dark sockets. His six foot body melting away like he's a snowman forgotten in the sunshine.

Watching for signals, I ask, "Wanna go outside?" His excited "Now now now!" tells me, thanks to Bob, that he wants to go out. I grab a sweater from his locker and drape around his shoulders. He can't help because his right side is a helpless burden now, like a full field pack would be. He depends on others for everything. This bewilders, frustrates, and angers him no end.

I grip handles of wheelchair and off we go. I know the way. Jim's pleased. We roll out to the courtyard. He directs me to a pavilion where he likes to sit. Other "Jims" are nearby.

I say, "How about ice cream on a stick? My treat!" His eyes light up . . . like a bonfire ember glows when a breeze whispers by. His excited "Now now now!" sends me off to the vending machine.

There's a special enthusiasm between us today. I remove the wrapper, put stick in his left hand, and tuck a paper towel under his chin. The look he gives me stirs memories of other times: football games, vaudeville shows, tin roof sundaes. Could he have special memories? Any memories? Does he know me? He gives me "Panna panna panna," and vaguely motions me to a bench near him. He's more relaxed than I've seen him in months. I sense a closeness like old times.

He finishes his ice cream. I take the stick, clean off his hand, wipe his mouth, dispose of the stick and towel. He studies his watch. He realizes he's due in occupational therapy in a few minutes. I can't tell if it's reflex action or awareness action. We wheel into the building and to his position at the worktable. I say quietly, "So long, my best friend Jim. May our Lord bless you and watch over you." He isn't aware I'm

leaving. He's busy cementing pieces of ceramic into what will be a hot plate.

Out in the crisp air, I wonder if Jim knows what fall is all about. I'm sure he missed summer.

It's a week later. Cold drizzly rain is washing fall away. Daubs of color left behind by the leprechaun are strings of muddied water. It's a fitting day to say good-bye to a best friend. The mourners have left. I'm alone with Jim and the cold drizzly rain. I struggle with a prayer made clumsy because of emotions I can't find words to express. A strange flush comes over me. A strange icy chill runs up my spine.

I say softly, "Jim . . . I know you knew me. Next time it's your turn to treat!"

Christmas

It's Christmastime
indeed indeed
and everywhere you go
you hear the kids exclaim
"We need a bright red sled
for snow."
And moms are baking
sweets galore
while dads
are trimming trees
and crowds are shopping
store to store
while clerks
are wild as bees
and everywhere that people are
a laugh or song will sound
the Christmas joys
from time afar
and love does full abound.

So give yourself
to all you meet—
your smile, your glow,
your fun—
"And may your Christmas be,"
you greet,
"a happy happy one!"

Many Things Are Christmas

Gentle curl of soft gray smoke
drifting from a red brick chimney
while lively flames dance happily
among the glowing logs . . .
these are Christmas!

Exquisite beauty of a snowflake,
a fragile whiteness by itself
yet a magnificent expression
of a mighty power
when snowflake after snowflake
fearlessly blizzard their way
upon the countryside . . .
snowflakes are Christmas!

Christmas means
different things to different people.

To some it means
there is a great living God above
who, in His infinite compassion
cares for us and loves us and
offers strengths
for the task of living.

To some it means
Jesus son of God was born this day
to help us find THE WAY.

To some it means
a great prophet was sent
to explain to us
the mysteries beyond
our understandings,
mysteries of love for each other
and respect and helpfulness
and the Power of Powers above
or beyond us . . .
such ponderings are Christmas!
May we all come to find a special
meaning of this day,
a deep wonderful meaning of Christmas
and have the courage and commitment
to carry these meanings
into every day of the year . . .
the friendly joy . . .
the caring one for another . . .
the sharing of the gift of love
with all we meet . . .

These many many things are Christmas!
Yes, indeed!

A Moment . . . a Breeze . . a Life

A moment.
Just a fleeting moment.
Was it just a fleeting moment you and I have shared?
A breath or so, a beat of heart as measured by a clock?
　　or have we rather searched the pages
　　Sharing thoughts with fools and sages,
　　Wond'ring, struggling, with the wisdoms of the
　　　ages?
Was it just a fleeting moment
Ticked off by a clock?
No! No! No!

A breeze.
Just a gentle breeze.
Was it just a gentle breeze that barely kissed our
　　cheeks?
A fluff of wind that softly blew then whispered into
　　nothing?
　　Or rather did we feel the gales
　　Blowing pirate ships of sails;
　　Or storms and calms from ancient days and
　　　age-old tales?
Was it just a gentle breeze
That whispered into nothing?
No! No! No!

A life.

Just a dot of life.

Is it just a plain old life, a dot of universe,

A dot to be erased one day into a kind of nothing?

　　Or rather's life created

　　Full of soul and not mere fated;

　　A heart and mind by God alone to be abated?

Is life a dot of universe

　　Erased one day to nothing?

No! No! No!